Letters to a Prisoner

Letters to a Prisoner

The Fight for Freedom

Oscar Valdes

Copyright © 2017 by Oscar Valdes

All rights reserved. No part of this publication may be reproduced, distributed, or transmitted in any form or by any means, including photocopying, recording, digital scanning, or other electronic or mechanical methods, without the prior written permission of the publisher, except in the case of brief quotations embodied in critical reviews and certain other noncommercial uses permitted by copyright law.

This book is a production of Editorial Madruga,
P.O. Box 78, Pasadena, CA 91102
You may visit the author online at oscarvaldes.net.

Library of Congress Control Number: 2017910255

Published 2017
Printed in the United States of America
PRINT ISBN: 978-0-9793558-1-3
E-ISBN: 978-0-9793558-2-0

Cover and interior design by Tabitha Lahr

For my parents and for my daughter

Preface

This is an effort to help you put your life in perspective. To remind you to never give up. To stir you to believe in yourself and your power to create.

I could only write these letters because you let me get close to you. You told me your story, shared your pain, the aching longing for another chance, and as you did, you let me into your heart and mind.

You have taught me a great deal. Yes, you. Stories teach and your story has taught me. The emotional intimacy that comes from telling a story has a strong effect on both the person who tells it and the person who listens. They humanize. They heal.

The acts you committed to bring yourself to prison were born out of moments when you were not connected to your humanity. You made the final choice to injure or be a party to it, but something had gone wrong in your life that set you up for the fall. That must be heard. That must be told so all can learn from it.

I will be hard with you at times. Even very hard. Do not despair. Do not throw away these letters. Put them down and return to them another time. Some things I say will be painful to bear but my intent is always to get you closer to your truth, for only in the fullness of the truth do we find our true freedom.

If there is an easier way, I could not find it.

Seek your truth and you will expand your power to choose.

And the victims, yours and mine—for we all have victims—may one day forgive us.

Letter to a Prisoner 1

So you're stuck in the pen, having to wear a uniform with the word Prisoner stamped on it, having to take orders, turn right, turn left, eating whatever they give you, and having to ration your toilet paper. And you shower when they want you to and if they want you to. You're wondering why you took the plea, why you didn't take a chance and go to trial. By now you're sure the DA bullied you. You know you're guilty, but you don't deserve the very long sentence you got. So what now?

You were hanging out with other gang buddies, just talking and smoking a joint—to your credit you had passed on the stick of Sherm that was going around—but then it got out of hand. "Let's go fire off a few," someone said. "Yea, let them know who runs this place," said another. You felt your insides cringe but you didn't say a thing. You chose to go along, though you didn't have to, did you? But you did. And now you're stuck in your cell and it's not pretty.

Morning till night you have to deal with stuff from other inmates, up and down the tier. You have to deal with guards, too. And you still haven't got all your property back. An officer told you he'd look into it but that was a week ago and you're still waiting. And you've got your legal work in the same bundle so you can't work on the appeal and the deadline is coming due.

The phone number you have in your head is not taking your calls. Or maybe you're missing a digit. It was with your property also. You should've memorized it but you didn't. And you haven't heard from anyone in the family and you wonder whether you ever will.

Your cellmate doesn't clean up after himself. He doesn't wash as often as you do and when he takes a leak he doesn't wipe off the pee he sprinkles on the ring of the bowl. On top of it, he loves to blabber on about this or that. Sometimes he slams his fist against the wall, just because. The man gets on your nerves. You're fed up. Some days, when your patience is running short, you're ready to flash on him. But not just him, you also want to flash on the fellow down the tier that said something about your sister, and you don't even have a sister.

When your cellmate gets to go somewhere, you feel the relief. You have the place all to yourself and you love the peace and quiet. You wish you could have more times like that. Alone. But then the thoughts come back. The regrets. The pain of not having stood up for yourself when you needed to.

Your mind doesn't pull any punches. Why did you quit school? "I wasn't doing so well, but why didn't I ask for help?" The thought haunts you. "I should've begged for help because if I had got it, I know I wouldn't have ditched to hang out with all the others. Little did I know that, just like me, they too had been giving up on themselves." Awful early to start giving up on yourself, you now think. Fourteen, fifteen, sixteen years old, even younger. Just when other kids the same age, in better schools, start to think of careers, you drop out. And you know it didn't happen overnight. It took time. And it's eating at you.

Moms and Pops were around but had their own problems. Or they weren't around. So you missed out on the parenting and it set you back. Anyway, no one ever told you—and if they did you forgot—that being free and staying free takes thinking and discipline. Thinking to figure out who you are. Discipline to hold on to your pain. Parenting was supposed to get you started on that. Then it would have been up to you to follow through.

But before you had a handle on it something went terribly wrong and there you are, stuck in that miserable, cramped little space, where it seems everyone is trying to push you down and no one is trying to push you up. If you had only thought of the consequences of your actions. You didn't and instead played dice with your freedom.

It's got to hurt.

But you know you can learn. You know because if someone provokes you now and calls you a name you don't just swing at them, instead you say to yourself that the person is a fool and has given up on himself. Even if he's wearing a uniform different than yours. And if someone comes into your cell and they have a shank or any other weapon, or drugs or anything illegal, then they have to go because you will not let another human being decide your fate. You did enough of that already.

You're grown up now, and you realize that you've got a mountain to climb. And you need to do it because you want to be free.

Letter to a Prisoner 2

Beginnings (Your Story)

You were feeling lousy about not fitting in with the kids who were doing well in school, and you said to yourself, "I don't want to deal with my feelings. I don't want to deal with what I have to do to catch up. Let me roll a joint instead." And you walked over to join the other kids who were in your same boat. Underperforming.

It was a critical moment, wasn't it? Looking back, a caring adult would've helped you face the facts.

The feeling that you were being left behind, that other kids knew the answers and got their homework done and you did not—that was pain. Not the pain from when you twisted your ankle but psychological pain.

A caring adult would've helped you give it a name. Helped you own up to it.

A caring adult would've insisted that when you didn't understand something you had to go right up to the teacher and ask for help. And if he was too busy, you then had to take it up a notch. You had to stand up in front of the class and say, "Attention everybody, I am having trouble with this subject. Is there anyone here who would like to take a moment of their time and be kind enough to lend me a hand?" And when your peers looked back at you, baffled at your audacity and maybe even snickering thinking you a fool, you would have looked them in the eye and repeated your request. And by doing so you would've been confronting your shame, not hiding from it. You would've been recognizing your need and putting it out there. You would've been saying, "I have my deficits but I want to better myself."

A caring adult would've helped you do that.

And if the teacher was worth his salt, he would have admired you for your courage and exhorted your peers to volunteer for the task. He would've said to your fellow students, "those of you who have greater ability ought to assist those who do not." Because when they do they are helping to lay down the foundation for a stronger community.

A caring adult would have told you that asking for help didn't mean the others were better than you, but that they had some advantages while you had yet to find yours.

You wish there had been someone around.

You had already seen a lot in your short life. You already knew what had happened to your cousin when he went to court for taking part in a drive-by and shooting someone in the arm. You already knew he had had trouble in school because like you, he had had no guidance either, and he chose to hang out with the wrong crowd and one afternoon got in the car with the older boys because he wanted to be cool and before he knew it they were handing him a gun and being told that if he wanted to really be cool he would have to take a shot at a house in the block coming up, a house where other dropouts that couldn't do the school work were hanging out and smoking something that got them to feel like they had no problems. For a little while only, because drugs don't heal the pain, they simply mask it. The dropouts at the home your cousin shot into, they weren't owning up to their pain, either. And when your cousin was handed the gun, for a brief moment he thought of saying no but then he felt that he needed to prove himself to the group, that he needed to belong because at school he wasn't cutting it. And later on, after the fact, when he went to court the public defender told him to plead guilty because if not he'd get life. And he got forty years instead. And after you heard the news you wondered why the hell your cousin's parents had not been summoned to court and asked why they had not provided proper parenting. But no, the court, made up of grownups, gave your cousin an ungodly, grownup sentence. And no, they didn't allow for the lack of parenting. The court of grownups let the grownups off the hook. They always do.

Letter to a Prisoner 3

Speak!

You wouldn't be in prison if you had learned to speak your mind.

You wouldn't be in prison if you had been able to say, "I don't feel well, what I'm doing looks wrong, how I'm being treated doesn't seem right, I hate falling behind in school, I want to be good at something, I don't know where my life is going, I am in pain, I am angry, I am sad, and I'm starting to hang out with the wrong crowd," and then had reached out to a responsible adult and opened your heart and mind.

You wouldn't be in prison if you had kept the big picture in mind and not given in to the pressures of the moment. If you had stuck up for yourself.

Mind you, it's not easy to do. Not easy to accept that we need help.

Learning to be alone with our feelings and thoughts is a big step in our development.

There's a recurring thought in all of us that quietly beckons, "Come discover yourself. I am here, do take a moment to do so. Please. You need you." We can ignore it, of course, but when we accept the invitation we will begin a dialogue with ourselves, and we will be on our way to finding out that we have a mind. And that is a beautiful thing indeed.

Our bodies, our minds, is all that we truly own. You may love another person and they may love you, and you are fortunate when that happens, but above all, you must endeavor to become your own person. Do that and you will be a better lover.

It is tragic to go through life without loving or being loved. It is just as tragic to go through life and not get to know yourself.

Those who willingly hurt others don't know themselves.

The irritations of everyday life will weigh upon you, as they do on all of us. Speak and you will lighten your burden. There is something about the way we're built that makes it necessary for us to share so we can heal. Don't fight it. Give in to it. Think of all the nurturing we need so we can develop into competent, self-reliant human beings. There is so much that can go wrong but when we get some of it right, what a terrific accomplishment that is. How inventive we can be.

Something went terribly wrong in your life and you are now in prison. But don't give up. You have lost your path for the moment. The dialogue with yourself shut down or didn't even start. When that happens we cease to see ourselves in the future, and we give in to the pressures of the moment.

Speak! And you will share what emotional maladjustments have stood in the way of your growth. Speak, feel, think! and you will be able to make sense of who you are. The sense of freedom will then come to you.

When you see a clinician, take advantage. Ask them to be a force for change in your life. Emotional and cognitive change. If you see a psychiatrist, don't just ask for medication, as important as that may be, but also ask for your behavioral prescription. Share something and ask for his opinion as to how you can improve your life.

At present there aren't enough clinicians to help with the work of helping you change, but don't lose hope. Be vocal. Ask for more help. Say you want to tell your story. And show that you are deserving by doing what you can to hold your pain.

You wouldn't be in prison if you had discovered you could. You wouldn't be in prison if you had discovered you had a mind.

Letter to a Prisoner 4

Assert your Difference

Look around. There is no one exactly like you, no one with your specific background, with your specific circumstances. You may share some qualities with others but the totality of you is unique. Someone has something you don't have? Don't let it distract you. Work with what you have and try to make the best of it.

Setting off on that journey is taking charge of your life.

You are in prison because you didn't take charge of your life. You let others influence you in a negative way.

Look for people who are improving themselves, who have a positive outlook on life, people eager to learn from their mistakes and move forward.

At any given time, there are people brighter than us, handsomer than us, stronger than us, abler than us. Nature sees to it. She does so because she loves diversity. Nature has a job to do—to preserve and advance itself—so it tries hard to put out as many variations as possible to achieve its goal.

You and I are examples of it. But variations cannot stand on their own. We need each other. All of us.

Don't try to be like anybody else. Accept your potential and strive to develop it. You can admire someone but don't idolize him or her. We are all flawed. Admiring someone is an invitation to learn. Be thankful that the person you admire has put effort into improving himself. You do the same.

Does everyone think that something is green but it looks to you like it is red? Pause. Don't buy into what others think before taking a moment to analyze. Believe in what you see and review your impressions. Maybe the group is right, but maybe not. Think. Respect your mind, respect your feelings. Be willing to be an individual.

Group think is bad news, outside of prison as well as inside. Dictators would not be in power if people thought for themselves. To stay in power, dictators keep people from thinking their own thoughts and exchanging ideas. But that is how we learn. That is the basis of our scientific and humanistic advances. If it weren't for the brave people who had the daring to assert their difference, be it moral, intellectual or physical, we wouldn't be where we are.

Dare to assert your difference. Dare to be you. Dare to improve yourself so you can make a contribution to your community.

Letter to a Prisoner 5

Prison Politics

Are you going to let them ruin your life? Why should you be expected to adhere to the party line—your skin color—when it comes down to confrontations between groups? In fact, why should group confrontations be allowed in the first place?

Someone big and bad picks on a weak member of another group? Let the authorities resolve it. It should be no different than if it happened outside of prison. Prison authorities should be protecting your rights as an individual, leaving you free to fight your most important battle, that of remaking yourself.

Be responsible for your own choices. Don't rely on the group to back you up. When a riot breaks out, all kinds of injuries are inflicted and sentences extended, affecting inmates not remotely connected to what sparked the confrontation.

If prison authorities are not doing their job of protecting your rights, then take up the matter in court, the same way you're expected to do when you're in the world outside.

I've seen many people come to prison because they took matters into their own hands and didn't call the authorities.

Prison politics is herd mentality because it favors irresponsible choices, as when individuals don't think through their actions and expect their group to bail them out. And as plain as this is, it takes some folks years to get it. But you have a choice to join in or not. And if you do, you have no one to blame but yourself. The fact that prison politics has been around since forever doesn't make it right. Racism has been around since forever, too.

Prison politics is game-playing. Violent games, mind you. It represents a complete denial of the obvious, that the better record you build for yourself, the less violence you have to your name and the greater the chance to get out when the law changes in your favor.

The fact that prison politics survives to this day is an example of the cultural poverty that prevails in prison, an example of the lack of mentoring, the lack of opportunities for improvement, the lack of forward thinking.

The various groups in prison today have more in common than they have as differences. A black, white or Hispanic man fails to develop for essentially the same reasons, and yet there you are adhering to a system of belief that aims to put each other down, to find ways of crushing and punishing yourselves, as if being in a profoundly deprived and toxic setting were not enough.

Prison politics is not only collective denial of the self but sheer madness. And yet it survives.

It's bad enough that all of you inherited your prejudices from your parents, now you're beating each other up over them. Why not try to build bridges instead? Why not try to find common ground?

If you join in with prison politics you've given up on your future. You've given up on your kids and your family. You came in for victimizing others and there you are doing it all over again.

So what are you going to do about it?

Letter to a Prisoner 6

Your Burden of Dysfunction

You didn't ask for it, you just got it. And it has weighed heavily on your life. The likelihood is that if you had not suffered such disruptive influences, you would not be incarcerated. Whether it's physical abuse, emotional abuse, sexual abuse, parental permissiveness or neglect, mental illness, learning disabilities, lack of intellectual and appropriate social stimulation, the effects of these influences can be devastating, the scars invisible, and the shame that comes with them such that it acts to prevent their reporting. Today, except for severe mental illness or a clear developmental disability, the courts barely acknowledge them as contributors in the commission of a crime.

There will come a day when researchers will find a way to measure and give proper weight to the various deficits that make up your burden of dysfunction, and it will help mitigate your sentence. But it will take time.

Don't lose heart. There are many people across this nation who, individually or as part of an organization, are working hard to see that every American's burden of dysfunction is acknowledged, prevented, or diminished. Guided by their humanity and compassion, they are now trying to persuade the rest of society that early traumas or deficits do impact development and consequently our choices. They believe that every man, with the proper help, can face his burden of dysfunction and work to reduce it.

And yet there will always be grey areas.

How much does your guilt owe to the pressures of the moment? How much to the earlier traumas and deficits that clouded your judgment? Unless you were mad at the time you committed the crime—mad as in psychotic—you are then fully responsible for your offense. But a crushing past ought to be given its proper weight in mitigating the sentence. And yet, sometimes, it will be hard to make a decision and be fair. There will always be grey areas.

You can help.

By being open about your story. Yes, you have a story to tell, and the sooner you find the strength to tell it, the sooner you will find your peace and your true identity. With that will come a greater sense of self-control, so that no matter how great your pain, you will learn not to give it to others but transform it instead. And as you do you will light up your path so that others will see.

An offense that results in an injury to a person is always a grave matter. The result of the interplay of various forces, genetic, upbringing, social, economic—it behooves us to take the time to sort things out, each and every occasion. A man's freedom is too important to not deserve our considered attention. We do not do this now. The underclasses, the poor and uneducated, fill our jails and prisons. The answer to this is not prejudice and neglect, but the hard questioning that aims to look at every facet in a man's development.

You must help.

Work on your mind and your emotions. The more you do, the closer you will get to being your own person. You will be pulling yourself up and keeping others from falling into the same trap, for they will see clearly where they tread.

And you will give meaning to your life.

Letter to a Prisoner 7

The Human Connection

There is nothing like it. Nothing beats it. You can hit the jackpot, but if you don't have that human connection then you're missing something vital. Without it we don't function well.

Think of the pleasures of friendship. You may be feeling down from the day's grind or one reason or another, and you talk to a friend about nothing in particular and you feel your burden suddenly lighten. You smile inside of you. Just a little, just enough.

We're social animals. We need that connection to thrive. You're in prison because you didn't have the right connection, otherwise you would've made better choices. Modern prison, then, ought to be filled with opportunities for rich human connections, so you can erase your deficits.

Connections can be problematic, but that's our task, to find solutions to the riddle, because that's where the purest form of energy exists. Everything that we've built is fueled by it. Call it human energy, call it love, we can't go far without it.

When we're hurt we build walls against it, sometimes impossible walls. But we lose in the end. The isolation gets us. It drains us and makes us poorer. We might even think that the world has turned against us—a bad sign, because it can lead us to think of striking back. And we dig ourselves deeper into the hole.

You can gauge how well you're doing in life by the quality of your relationships. If you have people in your life that you can talk with, people who value something about you, then you're moving along. It doesn't matter if you're not getting awards, it doesn't matter if you're not a big dog.

If, on the other hand, you have chosen to do the underworld thing, then you can be sure that isolation got you. You have given up on your possibilities as a human being. Sure, friendships with fellow dropouts can be a source of comfort too, but it's at the expense of your potential as a person. You're giving that up. You're choosing to roll dice with your freedom.

The best human connection is one that values you but doesn't bow to you. One where the other person values herself enough to disagree with you and call things as she sees them. Whether right or wrong. So long as it is civil. You want connections with people like that.

You want to have connections with people who have the courage to tell you you're a fool for wanting to do this or that. If you had had connections like that out there, you would not have set out on your path of deviance. You would not have sought the false comfort of drugs—because that's what they do, don't they, provide sham relationships.

Of course, we have to be willing to listen, to read the cues, to weigh what is being said, to be open to self-doubt. But it can save us a ton of grief and keep us from throwing away our lives.

You know how vigilant you have to be in prison, ever watchful. You know that, at any given time, in your unit or in the yard, there are people functioning at very different levels of development, people who give a damn and people who don't, people who want to renew themselves, who want to evolve, and people who have given up. You know that some may even be seething with freedom envy, because your release date is coming up and theirs is ten years away or non existent.

The person who does not give a damn, who is eager to pick a fight, to injure another, does not have the healing power of good relationships on his side. It is important to keep this in mind, because if you were to become his target, you will then defend yourself only enough to keep him from hurting you. If you were to knock him down as you shield yourself from his assault, you will not then jump on him while he is on the ground to finish him off. In restraint, you will be showing compassion and you will likely not be penalized or have your sentence extended.

A maturing man broadens his interpersonal skills as he evolves, deepening his grasp on what it is to be human.

Good behavior needs more rewards. Men who have shown a desire to improve themselves should be allowed the opportunity to establish meaningful relationships with responsible people in the community who are willing to contribute their time.

Letter to a Prisoner 8

Do You Want to be My Father?

Something happens in a child's life when he doesn't get to have a relationship with his father. He stumbles along, uncertainly, with the nagging sense that if the man never shows up, he'll have to embark on the quest to become his own father—and just how is it that you do that?

"Was it something about me, or something about him?" you ask yourself. Your mother, if she's around, can offer an idea. Or someone you came across and adopted, in your mind, as a person to fill the void.

If you are lucky enough to have a gift, some feature or ability that lets you shine and that others acknowledge, then that helps a great deal. But there's still the *what if.* What if he'd been around, how different would things have been.

Maybe he's been taking time off, or maybe he's busy with something really important, more important than me, you may say to yourself. Once he gets done with that he'll come back to see me. He helped bring me into the world, didn't he? Why would he do that and then walk away? I'm his son, my mom tells me I even look like him. A little. Why would he want to leave me behind, just like that? Why would he not want to teach me what life had taught him? And you say to yourself that Dad doesn't have to be a big shot, either, he just has to be himself, with whatever flaws he has. You just want him to be a real person, someone who will be there for you.

But for what exactly? There's so much going through your mind, so much you think you need from him, that you may miss what is obvious. You want him to be there for you just so you can talk. That's right. You want him to be there for you so he can give you a little of his time. And when years later you think back on it, it astonishes you that all you wanted, all you needed, was just that.

What for? To help you understand. Because when in the playground that afternoon, the stronger kid knocked you on your butt because you said something to him and you cried your heart out and wanted to kill him, you were so angry. You needed someone to hear your side, you needed Dad to break it down for you, so you would learn to accept the part you played in it.

That's sticking up for you. Giving you his time. Clarifying things. Does Dad have to go talk to the other kid's family? He may have to. But, for sure, you hope that he will tell you what you have to do different next time to better handle the problem.

Because if Dad gave you his time and explained and you understood, then he would have earned your trust. And when, another time, an older boy came up to you and asked you to go in the bush with him so the two of you could play a game and you had the sense that something was very wrong with that idea, then you would run to safety and then tell your dad about it. You wouldn't keep it to yourself. You wouldn't think that there was something wrong with you that you were asked to play the weird game. You would know that it is okay to tell your dad what happened. So he would break it down for you. So he would give you his time and you would understand.

And the more he would do that, the more you would feel that you could face the world without fear. The more you would understand the world as it is and that you have a place in it, and that you can help make it better.

Of course, Mom can do the job, too, and if she's all there she will do just that, be both Moms and Pops for you. But still you think that some things are for Dad to do.

But he was not around.

Now, in your cell, you wonder again how different things could have been if he had not left. You wonder if Dad had had a moment, just before he left, when he had looked at you and thought, "if I leave, he will grow up without a father." You wonder if Dad had had a moment, just before he decided to break the law or leave town or go on a drug run or whatever else was competing with you for his attention, you wonder if he had really looked at you and gave a moment's thought to how much you needed him. You, who he had brought into this world.

You wonder why he didn't sit down and look you in the face before he decided to leave or go gamble with his future, with his freedom, his life, and yours too. Sitting in your cell, looking at the four walls, you wish you could have told him what you know now. "Dad, when you helped bring me to this world, you were betting on your future. Now here I am. Don't run away from me, don't run away from yourself." Oh, if you had had those words back then. "Just be you, Dad, be you and hang around so you can stick up for me."

You wish you would've had the words to ask, "Did your dad leave you, too?" And you would've seen the answer in his face and you would've said, "It's okay if you don't really know how to be a dad, we'll work it out. See, if you're here for me, I'll be here for you. All I need is for you to be here, that's all, just for you to be here and give me a little of your time. I'm worth it, Dad. You help me become and you will become with me." You wish you had had the words back then, the words to stop him from going out on whatever it was that he went to do.

As you lie on your bunk, you wish Dad had told you his story, because if he had, you wouldnt've been there staring at the wall. If he had been around and you had talked and he had stuck up for you, he would've helped you come into your power as a feeling and thinking human being, and he would've come into his own also.

And it occurs to you now, that maybe Dad left because he didn't value himself, that he didn't think he had it in him to be the anchor that you needed.

"Do you want to be my father?" you ask, as you sit alone in your cell. And you can say the words out loud because your cellmate is somewhere else. But you're a grown man now and no one answers your question. And it becomes all too clear that you have to learn to be your own.

Letter to a Prisoner 9

Does Society Owe You Anything?

When you injure, maim or kill another human being you are, effectively, dropping out. You are acknowledging that you lost in the competition for survival.

Your actions set off two kinds of justifiable rage, the one from the victim and his family, and the other from the community at large, and you must be removed from society so that you will not injure again.

But deprivation of liberty should not mean deprivation of opportunity, for who's to say that an incarcerated man, given the means, is not able to transform himself into a mature and competent individual, capable of compassion and industry? If so, what is the point of keeping in prison a man who has evolved? Is he not another man?

Not investing in the emotional and intellectual enrichment of the prisoner amounts to denying that he has possibilities for future development, regardless of age and length of sentence. It represents additional punishment, beyond that which is called by the sentence.

What stands in the way of the offender not having access to opportunities to remake his life? Revenge.

The victim is entitled to the fullness of his anger, no doubt. He has been violated. Society, too, has been violated, and it stands in solidarity with its members, though they have not suffered in the flesh. But is this societal anger not overrepresented in the lengthy and cruel sentences handed down? Is it not overrepresented in the poor quality of legal defense that the underclasses—which fill our prisons—currently get? If so, then the Prosecutor's office is wielding freely, unopposed, the mighty sword of revenge in the name of justice.

So what could we do to tame that excess?

The victim should be empowered. How? By devoting as many resources as necessary for him/her to recover from the injuries as soon as possible. A victim who then heals from his wounds may well attain another perspective on his offender and come to see him as meriting forgiveness. If so, why not allow him/her, or family, if they so choose, the right to return to the courts to petition for a reduction in the sentence? Why shouldn't a victim who meets with his offender and assessed for himself that the culprit has evolved not have the option of asking the courts for a review of the original sentence, which may have been cruel from anger because of its proximity to the commission of the offense?

Mental health counseling would have to play a role in helping to bring the parties together. But wouldn't this act as a strong incentive for the inmate to redeem himself? Prison at present is bereft of these options.

The anger of the victim is, in principle, more apt to being processed, for he/she is a concrete entity that can be treated, whereas society at large is largely amorphous and vulnerable to a thousand influences—i.e. the impact of some in the press, television and films—when often they have not allowed for a full depiction of the offender's story and thus stirred public rage that goes unexamined. Collective anger of this nature has had enormous say in the deprivation of opportunity that reigns today in our prisons, though it has been countered to some extent by the noble activism of many civic groups.

But what can you, the inmate, do regarding media outlets which do not present a full picture of the offender and instead readily embrace polar opposites? Shun them. Do everything possible to avoid them. They do you no good. Do not forget that your principal task is that of remaking yourself so that you earn your forgiveness, and that is a huge task that requires your full attention. Look for positive stories, stories that inspire. "Shoot 'em up" stories of good guys and bad guys, though they may entertain, are not adding depth to your views and judgments. Treat your mind with great care. It can show you the path to freedom. The more you do for yourself, the closer you will get to feeling what your victim felt, which furthers your development and healing.

In time, the greater part of society will come around to the position that investing in your future is investing in all of its members. And then the phases an inmate would go through during his incarceration would be something like this:

First—Denial, minimization or avoidance of responsibility for the offense.

Second—Full acceptance.

Third—Interaction with the Victim, after offender and victim have gone through mental health counseling to address their needs and a meeting of the two parties is seen as possible and desirable.

Fourth—Resolution of conflict.

Fifth—Integration or Return to the Community.

Does society owe you anything? Some people think that it owes you nothing. I disagree. At the very least it owes you an environment that does not demean or brutalize you. When you come to prison, you bring already a burden of dysfunction, whether you see it or not. You failed when you injured, maimed or killed, and that is your lot to shoulder, but you should have ample access to opportunities so that you may remake yourself, simply because you are a human being. Even if you didn't treat your victim as one.

An enlightened democracy never ceases to strive for a greater depth of humanity. It is in its best interest, though reversals of course are not infrequent and sometimes lasting.

And so your plight remains a challenge to most of us, for what happened to you could happen to me.

"There, but for the love of god, go I."

Letter to a Prisoner 10

Time for a Prison Corps

Prisons have improved in their openness to the public. But more is needed. We must get closer to the prison population and be more vigorous in our interactions.

A Prison Corps would be made up of college-educated men and women of all ages, committed to the task of furthering the socialization of inmates by doing the following:

1) Assisting in the telling of the inmate's story. Why shouldn't the story of a man, whose life was so derailed that he caused injury to another, not be told in detail so that the rest of society can learn from it, so that our youth can better understand what goes into the making of a failed person? Provided the inmate is willing to tell his story, these accounts would be then compiled into books and sold to the public. Many of our offenders are poorly educated and have difficulty putting their

stories in writing. Prison Corps workers would act as biographers and editors. Doing so would transform the stories of men, festering in prison, into potential agents of change for society at large. Why should we get this critical information only through the media, with their own filters, instead of directly from the inmate?

What happened in the courtroom? What deals were made? How well represented was the offender? Was the performance of judges and lawyers decorous? Was the sentence appropriate? That is all part of the offender's story. Most often, those interactions do not find their way into the public arena. They deserve to.

2) Assist in the furtherance of the inmate's literacy and numeracy.

3) Through book discussion, build their critical thinking and judgment.

The more we know the offender in detail, the more we will be able to take effective measures to prevent crime.

The telling of these stories has the potential of enriching the dialogue needed to repair our judicial system.

Letter to a Prisoner 11

Drugs

It is the easiest thing to do, using drugs while in prison. You are often depressed, the weight of your poor judgment is taking the breath out of you, and you look around and want to give up. Maybe you have a good cellmate to talk with, but maybe you don't. Regardless, though, you have to confront the call of drugs, for it is a call to escape. To escape from you.

Drugs are big business in prison. They are always there. Can the flow be stopped? Of course it can. But it is not. There is a hierarchy in any group that is assembled. The ones at the top, think. The ones at the bottom choose not to. What do drugs do? Keep you from thinking. They may provide temporary relief from whatever emotional burden you're carrying at the moment, but in doing so they keep you from confronting your reality.

Because you're housed in large units, there is no differentiating the population by education, temperament, capacity for impulse control. So you're left to face whatever comes your way. It's not pretty. You can look at it as another form of punishment they didn't tell you about when you got sentenced.

Ideally, every inmate who feels the pressure to use drugs should be able to speak to someone in mental health so that the problem causing the craving is addressed. The guards test your urine frequently for drug use, but there is no real system in place to prevent the use. Given the magnitude of the problem, the frequency of offenses in which drugs have played a role, the violence connected to it, there should be a sophisticated program available to treat and research drug abuse. But there is not.

So what do you do if seized by the pressure to use? If you don't believe you have the strength to resist, then consider this. If you use, you are damaging your brain and surrendering your ability to think, which means that you are setting yourself up to be taken advantage by other people. Look around. See who your real friends are. Whoever is urging you to use is not a friend, even if they're giving you the drug for free.

If you're having to borrow money to buy the drug, then soon enough you won't be able to pay for it, and that carries consequences, such as a good beating. Or else you'll have to do favors for others, favors that you may object to, but because you owe money you're at their mercy. Use a needle and you are asking to catch a disease, like Hep C or HIV. If after considering all of the above you still want to use, then you have descended to a point where you don't give a damn about your life anymore. Using the drug has become the equivalent of a first step to committing suicide. A slow suicide, but suicide nonetheless. So why not step up to the door of your cell and ask the guard to call the mental health staff on duty? Your life is at stake. Slow suicide counts.

But you may not want to do this and instead just get high. Even though you're rotting your body you just can't resist. Okay, well, then you should know this. Substance use afflicts millions and millions of people the world over. And there are a lot of very bright men and women working to assist you. You may not know them yet but they are out there. Today, for instance, in opioid addiction, there is agreement that using medications to help you get off the drug is better than going cold turkey. You are less likely to overdose if the craving overpowers you and you use again, and less likely to contract HIV or Hep C. So please know that you are not alone.

And then there is this. Asking your relatives or your girlfriends to try to smuggle in drugs for you is pure sociopathy on your part. It is bad enough that you may want to do yourself in, but to entice others to put themselves in harm's way to bring you satisfaction is madness. And the same goes for selling drugs, for you are deliberately poisoning the minds of your brothers. In other words, mister, learn to deal with your pain and don't give it to others.

Letter to a prisoner 12

On Child Abuse

Prisons are filled with people who have been abused—physically, emotionally, sexually. There is not a single more disruptive force in the making of a person, short of starvation, than the abuse inflicted as a child. And yet, because the reports are made by prisoners—guilty of victimizing others—their accounts are not properly acknowledged.

Reports of child abuse by a prisoner are viewed with profound skepticism and often seen as the prisoner's attempt at minimizing responsibility for his actions.

Commonly, the victim of abuse is filled with such shame that he does not reveal the information. And so he endures it. He has a sense that his deviance is deeply connected to his painful past but he does not seek help.

Think for a moment of how difficult it has been for highly productive members of society to come out of the closet sexually. The weight of societal prejudice can be such that the person chooses to suffer the pain rather than disclose his preference. And these people have had at their disposal a wide variety of sources of gratification—professional and otherwise. Compare this to the prisoner. As a rule, he is poorly educated or struggling with learning disabilities, raised in a troubled household with a dearth of positive role models, or from early on exposed to drugs and an abundance of examples of deviance.

With that kind of backdrop, are the chances of adapting well to a demanding work environment not diminished? What are the chances of holding on to your pain when the outside pressures mount and you see yourself falling behind, not able to keep up with the competition?

The abused is likely to see himself as alienated—profoundly out of step, unable to join in with the world passing him by. Without the intellectual and emotional sustenance that strengthen character, such a man is less able to curb his impulses and delay gratification. Is it a surprise, then, that men in this condition are prone to err in their judgment?

Take sexual abuse. Having been victimized does not let you escape, it is with you constantly, nagging at you, pressuring you, filling you with shame for not having prevented it—how could you, when you were a child and trusting?—all the while ruthlessly demanding that you seek revenge. Revenge to lessen the shame and the guilt. One bold move on your part, one daring stroke of defiance (goes the illusion), and you can undo the damage.

Day in and day out, the expectation gnaws at you, like slow torture. Oh, if you could only pick your fights. But tortured minds are impulsive and easily misfire, and risky behavior becomes the norm. *One swift move and I will prove myself,* you keep insisting, while prison waits patiently, the frequent destination of the so-disposed.

The courts look upon these troubled backgrounds with skepticism. The weight of the offense crowds out consideration of the invisible scars. Against the brutality of the offense committed, how can you raise the question of such past wounds? The bearer himself does not want the wounds exposed, and no one looks for them. Instead, he longs to heal on his own, a last-ditch effort to escape scrutiny and save face.

But it does not work that way.

To heal you need a witness. And it cannot be the perpetrator. It has to be someone neutral at first, someone you convince with the telling and sharing of your shame. That's how the healing starts. By telling your story and seeing that someone believes it. Really believes it. It is curious with abuse, sexual, emotional, physical. You cannot heal yourself, you have to do it with someone else. Slowly, by convincing the one who listens of how your shame and pain came about, you regain the power that was stolen from you. Stolen from you when you didn't have a chance.

Did you enjoy the abuse at some point, while it was being perpetrated? If so, you have to say that, too, for it represents the height of the abuse, the abuser having persuaded you that his violation of your body resulted in pleasure for you. It is the abuser's triumph. And when you, the sufferer, the abused, are able to take your listener to that point, then you regain your full powers, for you have admitted to another person the fullness of your humanity. You had not yielded power to the abuser, you had been seduced and coerced, and you, with your story being told, admit to your frailty, and to the frailty of all human beings, including the one that you victimized and brought you to prison because you could not hold your pain. And you and your victim become one.

We are not there yet.

Present-day prison does not yet see the picture. It is bent on punishing—as in incarcerating without providing sufficient means for self improvement and healing—because it has not been willing to hear the whole story. The courts have not. The public at large has not. They have preferred to look the other way, preferred to think that the bearer of abuse, having abused others, should heal himself if he so wishes, and that living in a setting of cultural and social deprivation should be a powerful motivator to do so. But it degrades instead.

Beware of not telling your story. A story not told is a story at risk of being repeated.

It is not uncommon to see incarcerated men who have been found guilty of sexual molestation, who were victimized themselves as children. And you know how other inmates, not having yet examined their own stories, respond with murderous rage toward these offenders. Perhaps they identify with the children, if they themselves had been abused, and targeting the child molester promises absolution from their own shame. Or perhaps they identify with the victims because their childhoods were ravaged too. But violence will do nothing to mitigate their guilt or their shame. The mind is far more intricate than that. What it craves is understanding.

Letter to a Prisoner 13

Feeling Trapped in Your Personality

You know that neither your thoughts nor your emotions have helped you out. You kept making the same mistakes over and over again. Your thoughts didn't bring you clarity of judgment and your emotions didn't bring you inner peace.

Men are born to be free. And it is our obligation to ourselves to fight our fight, to assert our difference in the world while respecting that of others. It is our obligation to make the most of what we have in the world as it is. The very gifted, the very bold or very determined, get to live in it and change it. And if you are in that category, go for it. As an Indian sage once said, the universe will reward you for the risks you take on its behalf. But for the majority of us, it is the hard slog of adapting to reality, striving to become self-reliant, starting a family, and maybe one day distinguishing ourselves in some positive manner.

To adapt well to the world as it is, a man needs to take chances, sometimes big chances. But you don't take chances with your freedom. Not in a democracy. Even if the world is unfair, you play by the rules until you get a chance to change them.

When you used drugs, got into a gang or dropped out of school, you gambled with your freedom. And when you chose to hurt others you violated their freedom. And now you are sitting in a cell, stewing in your regret, with people telling you what to do all day long.

Why did you gamble with something as precious as your freedom? You didn't take a hard look at yourself and accept your difference. You didn't accept who you are, quirks and all. You did not connect with a centered human being that could have helped you sort out the big questions.

When you don't have a sense of who you are or who you can be, then it is hard to imagine what freedom is. "Play by the rules?" you said to yourself, and you answered, "Heck, no. I'm SuperDude, I can get away with it." All the while, though, you were covering up the nagging feeling that you were failing as a person. You were running away from that necessary confrontation with yourself.

Now that you are stuck in your cell, you are more likely to face yourself. But you can still find ways to evade that central task. You can pick a fight with your cellmate or the guard, you can develop a drug habit—anything to spare you the work of dealing with your life. All the while, though, you know you are not SuperDude. You know that SuperDude doesn't come to prison. You know that Super-Dude lives, comfortably, in the imagination of all those who don't want to face their essence. And deep down, you know that to grow up, you have to kick SuperDude out of your mind.

Because you offended, I know you did not get the proper help as a child. Even when parents are at home, they may not be at home. The key, protective ingredient in a child growing up is that he gets the sense, as early as possible, that he is capable of becoming a full human being. And for that he needs to have a caring, understanding, lasting connection to a centered person who is able to hold his own pain and transform it. And the child will learn to do it himself.

Every class in every school, from preschool to the end of college and beyond, should open with a one minute of silence, where we say to ourselves, "If I am in pain I will not give it to anyone else. I will hold it and deal with it. If I can't do it on my own, I will call for help." That simple. Every classroom in every school in the world. One single minute.

Some of our laws are oppressive. Take the Three Strikes Law. I think it is an instance of blatant, institutionalized cruelty. And it's been in place for more than twenty years. Twenty years where the greater part of society has looked the other way, not interested in addressing the fundamental injustice. Of recent there have been some changes, but all is very slow. And yet that is the world as it is, unfair, too often cruel but beautiful, too, if we can hold our pain and learn to process it.

You did not and I am very sorry. It is lamentable to see a grown man trapped in his mind and body, unable to exercise his freedom, his possibilities as a person, because he could not restrain himself to apply his energies to becoming a productive member of society.

But you can change.

Even if you are the bearer of the oppressive and suffocating pain of abuse, you can begin by stating what happened to you. You didn't ask for the abuse or the neglect or the lack of guidance that turned your life upside down, but that is your burden in life and you have to take responsibility for it. You can and you must. That is your lot. Your burden can take you to the edge and often does, but unless it drives you to madness, you remain responsible for the offense you committed. Unless it drives you to insanity, there is always a little daylight through which you could have asked for help, a little daylight through which you could have reached out to another human being. You did not.

So there you sit, with your thoughts and feelings weighing heavily upon you, sometimes crushing you. The thought of ending it all crosses your mind. The rage eats at you. Rage at yourself, at the world, at anyone who was able to figure out a way out of his predicament, like you did not.

No amount of taking it out on others is going to bring you back your freedom. No amount of shouting in the unit and cursing at the guards and at your fellow inmates. To bring back your freedom you have to work your way up. You have to build your personality, learn how to hold your pain and transform it into a positive force.

Can a grown man change? Yes and yes! So long as you're alive and willing, you can reinvent yourself. But you have to dare to open your heart and mind and work with someone to guide you through the journey. You have to dare to be free.

Letter to a Prisoner 14

Mental Health

If you were guilty of your crime, you need it. If you think you don't, then you're practicing self-deception, the same kind that led you to the path of deviance. "I can smoke that stuff and it won't mess with my brain. I can sniff that glue and I'll be okay." You won't.

Just as there is prejudice in society at large against mental health, so there is in prison. You're not born with prejudice. Our parents teach it to us. And that goes for all prejudices. But now you're stuck with it. And yet, something about asking for help with conducting your life seems hard, as if it were an admission of defeat. You may even be holding on to an excuse, as in "If such and such hadn't happened, if my partner in crime hadn't snitched, I wouldn't be here." But stuff did happen and there you are stuck in prison, with people telling you what to do all day long, away from your girl and your kids.

You are in prison because you didn't think, you didn't feel deeply enough and you refused to play by the rules. You refused to take on the world as it is.

If you keep making the same mistakes, you will be in prison longer. If you had trouble with your anger, you will continue to have it in the pen.

In California it has been only in the last ten years that mental health counseling has begun to establish a strong presence in prisons. It's been an uphill battle. Mental health is still learning how to best serve the inmate. The main obstacle has been dealing with its own bias against the inmate, the sense that there is only so much that you can change.

Why the prejudice against seeking counseling? Two reasons: one, it's hard to look at psychological pain, and two, it is awfully easy to lie to ourselves and say to the pain, "Catch you later, baby, when I'm not so busy," and then add, "Anyways, I'll do it on my own because I don't need anybody." But you're always busy and you know you can't do it alone, so it's downhill from there. Look, we can't grow up by ourselves. We need our fellow human beings. We need the care of others. That's just the way we're made.

You had a number of things go wrong with your life. What set you up for deviance was not your fault—you were not born to become an offender—but what happened later, you had a hand in. You didn't get the support you needed to get started in life so that set you up, but it was you who slammed your fist or pointed the gun or pulled the trigger or just went along for the ride. You did have choices. Unless you were insane—profoundly out of contact with reality.

Whatever happened to you, happened, and whichever ways you tried—over the years—to deal with what life presented to you, have now become entrenched. That's a big burden to deal with, and it's all yours.

But there is hope.

Sharing your problem can help you become a better person. It sounds simple, doesn't it? It is not. But that is where the road to redemption starts. There is no alternative. That is the path.

When you share, you're taking the first step to changing how you respond to stress and how you adapt to adversity without giving your personal pain to someone else. Working on your mental health teaches that. It does so by helping you to establish a dialogue with yourself, by assisting you in identifying your emotions, decoding your dreams, teaching the importance of restraint. Working with your mental health will help you discover that you have a mind. In a nutshell, it shows you how to value yourself. Yes. If you had truly valued yourself, you would not be in that cell looking at the four walls, with people telling you what to do all day long.

The love and understanding of a parent or a caring, guiding adult, does that. Gives you value as a person. You didn't get it at the beginning, as you should have, but you need to get it if you expect to be a free man.

Without valuing yourself, you will not care and you will offend again. In prison or outside.

If you thought you were a big shot because you pulled off a few robberies and didn't get caught, or ran drugs and got away with it, and it was only because of a fluke that you landed in prison, then you are sadly mistaken. You are not a big shot. You never were. If you robbed someone you endangered his life. If you sold drugs you were poisoning your brothers and sisters' minds. And slowly, one step at a time, you were painting yourself into a corner, giving up on your real possibilities as a human being, till eventually life caught up to you—the world, as it is, chased you down and got you.

Stuck in your cell, you now realize how short you had sold yourself. You had a brain but didn't use it. You didn't value yourself.

Mental health workers are trying to find ways to intervene earlier, to engage a person before they set off on a path of deviance, to engage parents so they can engage you in turn. It will take time, but there are presently thousands of researchers working tenaciously to find new ways to reach their fellow human beings. My hat off to them.

The central idea is to bring you aboard, to help you become someone who can make a contribution to the advancement of the human project. We will live our life spans and go back into the earth, but while we're alive and able-bodied, we ought to strive to be part of that effort, and we begin to do so when we learn to value ourselves. Value yourself properly and you will value others. They go hand in hand.

Not all in mental health will be able to help, but the majority will. Sadly, though, some still believe that because you crossed the line you are in a different species, instead of being a member of *Homo Sapiens*—from the Latin, "man with wisdom"—that you are instead part of a subspecies, akin to *Homo Insapiens*, man without wisdom, a being less evolved and incapable of rising to the higher station. But that is the world as it is now.

So if you happen to connect up with someone who truly believes you can learn to value yourself properly and thus better value others, hang on and give it your best.

Never forget that, regardless of what you did, if you make the effort to discover that you have a mind, you will be able to evolve. And even if your crime was such that you will not one day walk out of prison, with determined effort you may learn to fly out of it. Oh, yes, the mind that cultivates itself can grow powerful wings.

Letter to a Prisoner 15

Prisons Should Be Treatment Centers

From the very beginning we need to ask the right question: what went wrong with your life that you have done what you did? The rest ought to be doing what is needed to repair the damage and help you evolve.

I would rename prisons as Human Development Centers, and the clinicians devoted to the task I would call Adult Developmental Psychiatrists or Adult Developmental Psychologists or Social Workers. And the whole institution I would rename the California Department of Adult Development. CDAD for short. For it should be all about enlightened parenting, shouldn't it?

The only punishment must be the deprivation of liberty. The rest ought to be focusing on recovering your humanity, building on it and reconnecting you with the community. All with an eye to eventually bringing you and the victim together, so long as both are willing, so that the walls of anger and revenge are lowered, and the bridges of reconciliation and harmony are built.

Let us dare to imagine that we can do better than what we are doing now.

Letter to a Prisoner 16

Guilt

Guilt hurts. It presses down on you and darkens your mood. Sometimes it seems unbearable. Some try to run away from it, but it's not possible, for guilt never lets you go. When you're fully aware of it, however, you will find a new depth to yourself and you can move to a different stage of personal development.

You've heard of the expression, "No pain, no gain," as used in physical fitness. It applies to emotional fitness also. If you don't face the guilt, if you don't wrestle with it, it will influence your life in ways that undermine your best efforts. Guilt that has not been confronted will act to block your possibilities and mislead your aims.

Some people have greater difficulty acknowledging their feelings. For them the road to self-awareness will be tougher, but if the desire is there, the work can still be done.

When you confront your guilt, the image that you have of yourself will have to change. You will need to make adjustments for your darker side, your callousness, your insensitivity, your narcissism, your treachery, your meanness. But you will be doing yourself a favor, for it is all part of becoming human.

You're in prison because you violated other people's rights. You dismissed others. Devalued them. Dehumanized them. And as you did to your victims, you did to yourself.

Guilt can kill. When the pain is intolerable, suicide is seen as an option. But is it not also a shirking of responsibility to yourself and to the victim or family?

Guilt will not let you go but it can be transformed. In fact, it ought to be processed into a positive force.

Think of the harm you caused. Now think of what you can do to repair it. If you so choose, guilt that is faced and fully understood will become your engine of healing, the drive that will help you accomplish all that you must to remake yourself and honor your victim.

Yes, honor your victim. Your transgression means you are in debt to that person and to their relatives for the rest of your life. If you have maimed or killed, you will always be in debt, no matter that you completed your sentence, for that does not free you from guilt.

Owning up to your actions is the first essential step to transforming your guilt into a positive force. The other is to work to repair the injuries you caused, which means a sustained effort to contributing to the human project, to be kind and understanding to others and so ease their pain of living.

If you have grasped the depth of your guilt, it will not stand in the way of your new choices.

Letter to a Prisoner 17

What You Should Say to Your Son or Daughter

"I did what I did. I robbed, I injured, I hit a woman, I raped, I killed a man. And I did it because of this, A—B—C." You tell him the truth and only the truth. Anything other than the truth can lead to your son following in your footsteps.

You don't want your son to become your cellmate.

But you and the truth have had a troubled relationship from the start, so it is going to take a big effort on your part. If you had had a better relationship with the truth, you would not have dropped out of school. And you would not have chosen to use drugs. And you would not have chosen to hang around the wrong crowd. Even if the wrong crowd were your cousins or uncles and aunts. If you had had a better relationship with the truth, you would have been able to say to yourself, "They're blood and I love them, but they are not good for me. They are a bad influence on me and I have to stay away."

The secret to having a relationship with the truth is to value yourself. So you can look in the mirror and say, "I don't like what I see but I am going to do what it takes to fix it, for I must hold my pain." But if you didn't have the needed caring and understanding early in your life, then you got off on the wrong foot.

You don't want your child to do that.

So lay out the truth for him/her and they will know exactly what not to do. Embarrassed as you may be, you have to delve into your motivations. To get to their essence is going to hurt, because you are looking at raw emotions that you did not know how to process and led you to the failure that is hurting another human being.

It can be very hard to get to the truth. It is easier to say, "I was on drugs." "I needed to provide for my family." "I was hungry." "I was desperate."

Sharing the truth, examining it in detail, will fill you with shame but will make you stronger, for you will learn to own your pain, and as you do your judgment will improve.

It is very sad to see a man who is about to leave prison and is not able to speak candidly about his crime. Pressed, he may simply say, "I've learned my lesson."

When you present the truth to your son or daughter, you will be empowering them. There will be no chance of their saying to themselves, "my pops is a 'bad' dude, real tough, and one day I'm going to be like him." Instead he will see you as a troubled man who found the courage to face himself. And you will be giving him a gift that he will treasure for the rest of his life.

The present American prison is not a propitious setting for this discovery and revelation. The units are too large, mainly designed for warehousing. Mental health is still viewed with suspicion and lacking in independence from custody.

Improvements to the setting should go in the direction of much smaller units, housing twenty or twenty-five inmates, one man to a cell, men selected by their willingness to learn to control their impulses and their motivation to change. All daily activities to be kept separate from other groups, including dining, education and rehabilitation.

This arrangement holds the promise of reducing violence between inmates and of deepening the quality of their rapport with both custody and mental health. It would also allow for the inclusion of custody in the therapeutic process, for the setting would be, in effect, a therapeutic community.

The greater the individualized care, the higher the likelihood of significant gains in the process of personality repair needed to move the inmate past his offense and help deliver to society a productive citizen.

Many of these smaller units could be grouped together in an area enclosed within a secure perimeter. Inmates who distinguished themselves by their efforts would be eligible for promotion to higher-functioning units. Those who failed to adapt would be sent to lower-functioning levels with different therapeutic approaches.

An effective system of rewards needs to be put in place, with satisfactory behavior promptly reinforced. Examples of rewards are greater frequency of family visits, access to opportunities for greater skill acquisition, and contact with the community.

The present design of housing inmates acts as a detriment to rehabilitation and is a clear obstacle in the path to self renewal. It generates violence, decreases the acceptance of mental health and its transformative powers and promotes drug use. It needs to change.

Letter to a Prisoner 18

Valuing Ourselves

Mostly it is unconscious, and if it is positive we have nothing to worry about. We will go through our day without incident, and if one were to occur we will have the appropriate response.

But if our self-valuation is faulty or negative, it puts us at risk. For instance, a man may think that his occupation is not suitable for his abilities, or if suitable he is not being properly compensated. A man in such state of mind is vulnerable. If in the course of the day, he were to be slighted or offended, he might overreact and make matters worse, for when you overreact you are giving the other person power over you.

When we step out of our homes we are open to interacting with a thousand people who are at various levels of development or personal satisfaction. Some may not be able to hold their pain and are eager for any opportunity to pass it on to someone else.

You may have had an argument with your wife that morning, just before stepping out into the world. Or an argument with your child. If you ended up not feeling at peace with the outcome, you are liable to carry that leftover with you. Be mindful of this, because it puts you at a disadvantage. If you then get on the freeway and someone cuts you off or commits some other offensive behavior and you are not on your toes and remember that you left your home in a vulnerable state, you could easily overreact. If you do so, you are giving that other person power over you.

Men are often tangled up with issues of dominance, which leads to a narrow safety range in everyday transactions. In prison, it gets even narrower.

You're going down the street and another man is coming in the opposite direction. You glance at him. If you were to linger just a little, the other person might read other meanings from the exchange. He might see it as a power challenge. Or as an expression of sexual interest, which may not be welcome. Some men simply do not glance at another man's eyes, to avoid the issue altogether. However, if that day you had stepped out of the comfort and safety of your home and had matters unsettled in your mind regarding spouse, children or work, your self-valuation may be diminished, and you would be more likely to try and stare at the man coming toward you. That may give you the feeling that you are recovering some of your power, but you do not know what the other person is going through. If his self-valuation happens to be low or negative, he may be eager to find some way to reassert himself and you just might have handed him the opportunity.

Before you leave your home, check to see what your

self-valuation is. If it is negative, you are at risk of displaying risky behavior. Just be aware.

A word about body type. Nature did not create us equal. Everyone has more of this and less of that. In confrontational sports, we've agreed to match people with similar physiques, as in boxing, wrestling or judo. In the world at large, though, we are on our own. Physical power being a fact of life, those who have it may use it to intimidate, dominate or take advantage. But you have your own power, too.

In prison you have fewer options to be out of the range of a physically powerful person intent on preying on you than in the outside world. Neither are you offered suitable protection. It is therefore critical that your self-valuation be accurate. This process begins with reminding yourself that your body is not to be violated under any circumstances. You have violated other peoples' rights, which is what landed you in prison, but asserting that your body is sacred—not to be messed with by anyone—is a crucial step to your healing. And to understanding what you did to others.

Even though you may have less physical power than another person, you have a brain and a mouth. The brain is your organ of survival. As the seat of your thoughts and emotions, you use it to assess any situation for danger. It could be that the more powerful person is a kind individual who would never want to take advantage of you, but until you're dead sure of that, you do not put yourself at risk. That is your right and your obligation, no matter what you're in prison for. That includes not allowing yourself to be put in a cell with someone stronger or more dominant than you, or even accepting a visitor in your cell, during day room, that you don't know or feel comfortable with.

You just do not allow it. Anyone trying to boss you is not a good sign. Stay away. Get out of range. That is using your brain. I cannot insist on this enough. You must choose who you associate with.

If you are thinking poorly of yourself, you could easily lower your guard and think you need the protection of a stronger man. Don't do it. No matter how small you are, physically, you have a brain and a mouth. Assess each and every situation, and if you don't like it, get away. Use your brain to assess, your mouth to say "stay away from me."

Beware that, sometimes, there may be unconscious forces at work, such as self-loathing, that may impair your judgment and lead you to being trusting with people you don't know, or to using drugs with them. Don't do it. Self-loathing needs to be dealt with in mental health. Regardless of what you did, if you accept your share of responsibility, your time in prison can be the start of a new life. Having someone take advantage of you is not. Assert the sacredness of your body. Nobody messes with it. As you get closer to yourself, you will get closer to what your victim suffered or is suffering.

Avoid using weapons to protect yourself. The moment you think of these options it means you're not using your brain or your mouth. Those are your real weapons. If you don't think you have a brain, then talk to mental health. They will help you find it. Yes, sometimes we humans have a way of misplacing it. Mental health will help you find your mouth, too. You need your mouth in prison as much as you need it outside. If you had used your brain and mouth properly you would not be in prison. Having weapons in prison is a recipe for adding time to your sentence. Do not do it.

Just as exercise keeps your body strong and healthy, so

does thinking help to keep your brain fit. You need it to assess the people you come across, to find out if they're committed to enhancing their lives and will not disrespect you or try to use you. If you can sort that out, then good friendships are a real treasure. A good friend will tell you what you do not want to hear. If you find someone like that, keep him. Of course, the expectation is that you do the same for him. Think ahead, anticipate. The more you do, the less likely it is that you will ever deliberately harm another person.

Before you leave your cell, check your P.E.P.—your Psychological, Emotional and Physical status. On a scale of one to ten, you'll rarely be at a ten—unless you're on drugs, which is why I call drugs the Great Liars. By doing your self-valuation check, you will be acknowledging what you need to be mindful of. Am I aware that others have their own difficulties? Am I aware that I am not the center of the universe? Am I aware that envy can affect my judgment and actions? Am I aware that I ought to always be courteous, with men and women alike, whether I perceive them as superior or inferior to me? Even if they are not courteous with me. Am I aware that to better live in the present I have to think of the future? Am I aware that I have to hold my pain? If I suspect that a friend double-crossed me, or my girlfriend likes another man, or a woman, do I think about the consequences of rash action on my part? Am I aware that physically I am not King Kong? And if I am, that I must never underestimate a man of smaller size? Am I aware that physical confrontations are best avoided unless my life is on the line—and even then, check again. Men who have suffered physical, emotional or sexual abuse are prone to be paranoid. Beware.

Make friends with your future. See yourself, regardless of age, as a developing human being. See yourself as someone who can always improve, and who must do so to better enjoy the life you have. Whether you have a set date to leave prison or not. Make friends with your emotions and your thoughts and your dreams. That is what you have. Work with them. If someone has more than you do, acknowledge it and move on. Work with what you have and make it count.

Healthier environments have less social friction. As best you can, surround yourself with positive people. If you find yourself in a setting with high social friction, check your P.E.P. You know that there are inmates who were just about to finish their sentences and ended up getting in trouble and extending their stay, sometimes only days before they were to be released. The likelihood is that they had not dared to examine their unconscious. Don't let it happen to you.

Every time you don't show restraint, every time you don't hold on to your personal pain, you are letting others have power over you.

We are all vulnerable because we're human. The task is to handle our vulnerability.

Letter to a Prisoner 19

Guards

You've got to learn to live with them. Like the rest of us, some are more insightful than others. Some have great interpersonal skills, better than some doctors and clinicians, and are mindful of the fact that something went terribly wrong in your life and that it had a profound effect on your choices. Others may think they are there to add to your punishment, forgetting that the only punishment should be the deprivation of liberty and no more.

You've got to learn to live with them. Keep foremost in your mind that you have been an impulsive man and you need to learn patience. Guards who have to interact with prisoners are usually outnumbered and find themselves under a great deal of pressure. Do not push their buttons. They are people.

To prevent a confrontation with guards, follow this simple rule: Treat them as you would like to be treated yourself.

Guards can make life easier for you. The vast majority want to get through their day without an incident. They are not what brought you to prison. You did. But if you do catch a guard being unfair to you, then say so in as polite a way as you can. Make allowances for human frailty. We all are flawed.

Never forget that you have a brain and a mouth and you need to rise above the pressures of the moment and think of the consequences. If you get into it with a guard, you are, likely, not seeing yourself in the future. You are letting the pressures of the moment do a number on you. Beware. It takes two to tango. Make sure you check yourself to see what you are bringing to the conflict.

I have seen many inmates who have extended their sentences significantly because they would not observe the simple rule listed above. A history of being aggressive landed them in prison. Always on edge, trapped in their character pathology, they seem unable to lift themselves to see the big picture. Instead they stay stuck in the moment.

Learning to pull back is critical.

A great deal has gone wrong in the making of a trapped man's personality, but running his mouth is not going to undo what forces shaped him. In present-day housing, with people of diverse backgrounds all bunched together, it is frequent that these trapped men stir up unrest. Others, stranded in their boredom, eager for excitement, may even egg them on. But the trapped man driven to relentless confrontation always ends up the loser. The joke is on him. He just doesn't get it.

These men belong in separate units where they can get specialized care—otherwise it is easy to give up on them. In a modern prison, from the outset, all prisoners should be assessed for impulsivity and ranked accordingly. One thing is a paper test when you first come through Reception; another is the advantage of close observation. Guards can make an important contribution in this area. They have experience in spotting the inmates who are overly confrontational.

An inmate neighborhood that is frequently disrupted by a few confrontational people is more likely to have other inmates adopt that style, which raises the level of stress for all concerned, leads to injuries, fosters drug use, and ends up requiring more emergency mental health interventions and more medical care in general.

Do not let others run your program. You need to focus on the changes you need to make to regain and keep your freedom. That is your number one job.

Letter to a Prisoner 20

Are You Institutionalized?

It comes in slowly, sneakily. But the effects are devastating.

You are becoming institutionalized when you think of settling a dispute with a knife. When you agree to be part of a drug deal, or when you ask a relative or a girlfriend to smuggle in some drugs for you.

You are becoming institutionalized when you target a child molester. You can't wait to inflict punishment because you think it will get you some points with the rest of the inmates. In fact, it takes greater courage to acknowledge that the child molester has his own burden to carry, and if you were molested yourself, how do you know that the child molester was not a victim, too? What gives you the right to pile on to his problems?

You are fast becoming institutionalized when you can't stop blaming custody. Any shortcoming on their part is cause for you to heap blame on them. Take a moment to examine what you are contributing to the conflict. Why not learn to work with them? Remember, treat others as you would like to be treated yourself. Do what you're told and hold on to your pain. Think others will call you a snitch? Maybe they are caught in "group think," cannot extricate themselves and want you in on it. As the saying goes, misery loves company.

If you think that challenging the staff is going to improve your standing in the unit, then you're the loser. You can't win that one, and you're giving them your power. Yep, what little power you have, you're giving it away.

Try to look at establishing cordial relations with custody as a challenge. It will help you practice your social skills. You'll need them when you get out, when dealing with parole, when stopped by the police. Having good relationship with staff does not mean you're losing your self-respect.

You are becoming institutionalized when you make fun of those who are choosing to utilize what mental health counseling has to offer. Check to see if you're envious that they have the guts to ask for help.

You're becoming institutionalized when you're not working on your appeal, not making every effort to find better legal representation, when you're not reaching out to family and friends, when you get angry at them easily. Don't chase them away. You need them.

And, of course, you have become fully institutionalized when you wake up in the morning with a big smile on your face, look around and say, "I love it in here. It's cool."

Letter to a Prisoner 21

The California Prison System and the Mental Health Bureaucracy

The future of the system lies with Mental Health, but we have to vastly improve how we go about our work.

There is Face Time (FT) for the inmate, and there is Paper Time (PT) on the inmate. At the time of this writing, Paper Time far outpaces Face Time, and that is not good for the work that needs to be done. Face Time needs to be on top. Always.

A colleague of mine once asked, half jokingly, "What happened to the paper reduction act?"

The urgent need is to spend the most time possible treating the inmate to help him become a socially competent individual. The need is not for producing mounds of redundant reports to satisfy the legal department.

The ratio Face Time over Paper Time, FT/PT (including computer time), should be something we measure and do everything possible to increase. I propose that it be at least equal to 1.66—if you work eight hours, five hours should be FT and no more than three for PT.

The legion of supervisors we now have should be doing everything possible to increase the quality of Face Time. They should be experts in therapy and should be spending the majority of their effort helping the clinician improve his ability to interact with the inmate, while reducing the forms that need filling, not adding to them.

The main reason this is not done today is that there is not a clear idea of what to do with the prisoner. A significant proportion of staff and administration do not believe that the prisoner can truly change. There is no emphasis on research. There is no effort to compare the available treatment methods to see what works best.

Which brings me to Creative Time. Modern prisons should be settings devoted to discovering and designing new ways to improve behavior. We should be producing articles and scientific papers on the subject. You have in front of you—unless you're hiding in your office burying yourself in reports—a mass of human beings whose common denominator is that they have failed to adapt to the complex demands of society, a mass of people who disconnected from their humanity and need to be reconnected. But if you dismiss them as antisocial and are not actively trying to delve into the wrecked humanity that lies just under the surface, then you're wasting everybody's time, including your own and the taxpayer's.

Clinicians who dare to think and are given the opportunity to flesh out their ideas will come up with new possibilities. There are many talented people working in prison today that, if given the opportunity to express their creativity, will rush to do so. But that is not presently encouraged. And we are wasting their potential.

We are also wasting the creative potential of guards. They help keep us safe, but they will also be able to make important contributions if we include them in the treatment process.

Punishment should be only about the deprivation of liberty. It should not be about banishment and warehousing, and it should never be about depriving a man of the opportunity to grow past his misdeeds.

Prisons need to be actively engaged with the victim and the community.

One model to explore would be that of allowing clinicians who treat the victim to come in contact with those who treat the offender, so as to find options for improving therapeutic approaches. Some victims could even be treated in clinics located on prison grounds.

Monetary bonuses for clinicians who distinguish themselves in their work should be allowed.

A word about medications. They do wonders. A bipolar, schizophrenic, depressed, or overly anxious inmate needs expert pharmacological intervention in addition to relationship therapy. But because of the setting that most inmates are now housed in and the tremendous stresses they endure, the need for medication is greatly increased. And so too the likelihood of substance abuse and its horrible consequences.

Letter to a Prisoner 22

A Journal for Clinicians

A monthly journal, where clinicians would contribute case reports, would stimulate scholarship among clinicians and raise the level of discourse. The more we do this, the more effective we will be with the inmates and the sooner they will find their peace. Of course, the identities of the inmates would have to be disguised.

And why not allow this journal to be shared with victim and inmate alike, with custody and the public? A small fee would help offset costs.

A journal for clinicians would be a step towards enabling all concerned to better hold their psychic pain so it can be transformed instead, and when transformed results not in an injury to another but in a gift, a gift to the human connection.

Letter to a Prisoner 23

Family

You need to keep in touch. Whatever happened to you that you veered off onto the path of deviance, you must try to understand. But connecting with family is not about placing blame. It is instead about learning to work together so that remedying actions can be taken.

If you did not commit a crime against your family, you must do everything possible to maintain communication. If you have children, you must make every effort to stay connected. I think it is a grave mistake for the spouse who is out there to block a dialogue between you and the kids. Of course, depending on their age they'll need guidance, but open talk that speaks the truth is the desired goal.

You were not born to be a killer or a thief. Something happened along the way that took you off the road toward your full development as a human being. By speaking the truth to your children, you will be doing what you can to keep them from repeating your mistakes. Sadly, it happens.

It is not uncommon to see various members of the family in the same prison.

If you committed a crime against your family, then you have to wait until you have done the work of redeeming yourself. And then you get on your knees and ask for forgiveness. Whatever the obstacles, though, do not give up. Keep working to remake yourself.

Prison is too grim not to make every effort to keep in contact with your relatives. Family gives hope. It can be a source of open affection, something which is in short supply in the pen. Men who stay in touch with relatives do better than those who don't. They are less likely to give up on their future, or to be a party to violent behavior or drug deals. They are more likely to be working on their cases to find flaws that could result in reduction of sentences or trying to get more effective legal assistance. They are more apt to stay focused on their recovery and less prone to being distracted with the everyday grind that devalues life.

Be patient. It takes time for relatives to get to visit.

There ought to be the option of family reconstruction. Expenses made toward this objective would be offset by a decrease in recidivism and parole violations. Investing in family reconstruction would result in a protective effect both for the offender and the community as a whole.

The offender gets the sentence, but he comes from the matrix that shaped him. Just how committed was that matrix to delivering a productive citizen? How responsible were the component members? Family reconstruction would offer the option of repairing the ties within the matrix, or keeping the existing ones from deteriorating.

An offender in prison who is disconnected from family

is at high risk of prolonging his sentence. Family reconstruction would help decrease the risk and the costs, human and economic, of incarcerating someone for the long-term.

Connecting with family eases the sense of being alone, alleviates feelings of insignificance, and helps you endure the pain of living.

Letter to a Prisoner 24

Mentoring

Nature may assign us different potentials, but so long as we put forth our best efforts to fulfill it, a sense of dignity will come to us. And when it comes, others will see it, and you will find someone to love and someone who loves you in return.

You will not harm others deliberately, you will not come to prison, and you will be free to live your life.

Envy is your enemy. Accepting your difference is your friend. Doing the best you can is your freedom.

Mentoring acts to facilitate the fulfillment of our potential, and it ought to be started as early as possible during a man's incarceration.

Imagine the possibilities of matching men or women who have faced and overcome adversity with young men or women who have failed to do so. It allows for concrete, palpable opportunities for positive identification, particularly if the interactions take place over a period of time. Mentors would describe their hardships and the world they work and thrive in. Mentors don't have to be stars, but men and women from all walks of life who've been tenacious at becoming the best they could be. This type of interaction serves to broaden the minds of inmates and remind them that they too can be part of the larger world if they apply themselves.

The Prison Corps I mentioned in an earlier letter could help search for mentors and nurture their relationships.

There are rules to follow in order to be included in our society. The inmate has violated them. But if he learns the rules he ought to be allowed back in. A democracy must be welcoming in this regard or we risk alienating significant portions of it, which is not in our best interest.

The case of today's homegrown terrorist shares elements with this concept. He perceives himself as alienated from the world he lives in and wishes to destroy it. He obviously failed to process his pain and instead chose to give it to others. But we must grow wiser at spotting when and where to intervene, so that we can lay down stronger bridges for inclusion.

With the disaffected there's no other option but to remind all concerned that an evolving democracy must stay an engine of opportunity and freedom for all.

Letter to a Prisoner 25

Before You Leave

Take stock of what you've accomplished. Beware of freedom envy.

As you well know, there are people who have not done their homework and who are envious of your going home. They will try whatever they can to get you to break the rules so you can stay in prison and keep them company playing dominoes. It is perverse, but you know it happens. If you need to lock it up and stay in your cell as your exit date nears, do so. So what if you don't shower for a couple of months?

Other inmates may come to you and ask that you give them a hand with hiding some dope, or a weapon, or help them settle a dispute. You must kindly decline, each and every time.

Real friends will be looking out for you, giving you warning that something might be coming your way and to stay clear. Real friends want you to get out of prison.

If someone attacks you, do only what you must to keep yourself from getting hurt. No more.

If someone provokes or insults you, by all means stay calm. Keep telling yourself that the person insulting you is a fool, and that you will not give up the power you have worked so hard to earn, the power to leave prison. Do not give it away to a fool. Do not give it away to anyone.

The moment you make up your mind to remake yourself and to work relentlessly to get out, begin an internal dialogue. Repeat to yourself daily that you have a future, that you will be free, that you are transforming yourself into a person that does not deliberately hurt other human beings, that you will overcome every obstacle, no matter what the length of your sentence.

Give yourself a new middle name, "Freedom." So if you're Stan Goodbrue, you will now be Stan "Freedom" Goodbrue, and so on. Invent whatever works for you, but the point is the same, to always remind yourself that what you do every day counts. Every decision you make has an impact on your freedom.

If you have a problem cellmate, don't wait for things to get out of hand. Anticipate. Think ahead. Start looking for someone more compatible to swap with. Do your homework. Try to work things out, but if the other person doesn't want to cooperate, clear out. Do whatever you have to do. Refuse to go back in the cell or declare that you need to see mental health as an emergency, and if no one's listening, then say you're suicidal. You do not want to be the story of the next day. "Oh well, his cellie strangled him. It happens. This is prison." And no, that was not part of your punishment, to be killed by your cellie because that is prison.

Do not be a victim. Take charge of your life. Remember your victim. Change your life.

As you near your release, you may get help from the state for the transition out, or you may not. It helps enormously to have a place to go to, which is another reason to stay in touch with your family. Not having a place to stay is an invitation to return to prison right away. Regardless, if you're determined you will succeed.

Letter to a Prisoner 26

Your Core

We all have the seed for one. The task is to nurture it and embrace it, as we do. The earlier the better, for it has a protective effect on development. It will keep us out of trouble and give us a sense of direction. What interests you? What moves you? What are you good at? What seems to come easier?

You know you're growing your core when you don't get easily distracted by other people's accomplishments. You may admire them, but you don't just put down what you're doing and go try to be like them. Instead, you recognize your difference and invest in it.

We cannot be like the person we admire. That is their identity. You need to find yours.

A person you admire can inspire you, and you may decide to follow into the field where they made a name for themselves, but you have to be sure you have the ability to persevere on your own. Without perseverance you have no chance of success.

After the excitement of being inspired by someone starts to fade, then it will be just you and the work to be done. No one else. Just the two of you. So if the work itself doesn't light your fire, then you will not be able to sustain the effort needed to succeed.

The person you admire, and who inspired you, put a lot of work into his quest. I can assure you that he/she had times when things were not going well, and still they endured. They took stock of what they had and then bet on their belief that they had the ability to overcome whatever difficulties got in their path. They sought competence, even excellence, but not stardom. They knew, or soon discovered, that they had no control over that.

Doing something well is its own reward. If others applaud, terrific. But don't count on it. At the end of the day, when you have only yourself for company, it will be what you think of yourself that will bring you peace. Are you going after what you want? Are you pursuing what you love? Are you exerting yourself fully? Are you striving to assert your difference?

In today's world, with the flood of news and visual media washing up at our feet every day, we come across a multitude of people who have accomplished worthwhile feats. Thank them from the bottom of your heart for their contribution to the world and get back to your own struggle.

There is no guarantee that you will ever be in the news like they are, regardless of how hard you work. So let that notion go. What you do have control over, so long as health permits, is the kind of energy you put toward your chosen goal. Persevere in your task and one day, competence, if not excellence, will become yours. And with that, the sense of a life well lived.

Dare to explore yourself. Admire others and learn from them, but don't be a slave. Be you. You have a world to discover and it may take a lifetime.

Letter to a Prisoner 27

After You Leave

Do not be afraid of your freedom.

Some people are, don't own up to it, and end up screwing up so they can return to prison. Yep, for some people, prison is safer than the world outside. Sad but true.

Be wary of old friends and acquaintances that you have lost track of. Just a reminder: if they didn't drop you a note while you were in the joint, then they may not be true friends. Caution.

Say that an old buddy recognizes you as you're walking down the street, two days after you're released. He stops the car, gets out and tells you how much he's missed you. "Glad to see you, bro. Wow, I knew you could do it. (You've just spent thirteen years in prison.) Say, I'm heading to the beach, a little party, you want to come along?"

You haven't been to a party in thirteen years—in fact, you spent the decade of your twenties in the pen. You look at the car and there's another dude you don't know inside and three women flashing you the smile. The old buddy sees you checking out the ladies and says, "Bet you haven't seen none of it in a while, have you?" He smiles.

So what do you say?

You pass.

Here's why. You haven't seen your old buddy in thirteen years and you don't know what he's been up to. What you don't need is for you to get in the car and then twenty minutes later be stopped by the cops because the car was hot and then for the officers to discover that your old buddy had a gun under his seat. And to boot, it is your luck that the gun could be traced to a deadly shooting a week before. Get the picture?

Say that you're desperate to be with a woman, and you connect up with one and you go to her pad, and you're getting some action, and suddenly she stops you. "Baby, I didn't tell you this, but I got a weakness for a little meth, just a touch, and I forgot to get some yesterday."

You've tried meth but haven't done any in ten years, because you know it blows out your brain cells and you need what you got to make it in the world.

"Honey, I shouldn't be doing that…"

"Oh please baby, do me this favor and I promise you'll have the best sex you've seen in your life."

You hesitate but you know you want it.

"Baby, my connection is just around the corner."

So what do you say?

You pass again.

Why?

Because it will be your luck that they're running a sting on the dope dealer and you will walk right into their hands.

Or the other so-called friend that learns of your release and needs to collect a debt. He looks at you and says, "Man, it's great to see you. As they say, you can't keep a good man down. Welcome to the world. Say, Devon, I'm running a little business on the side and this fellow here is not paying up. I need a guy like you, all buff, muscles ripping, to just pay a visit and remind him that business is business. Get my drift?"

You hesitate.

And your so-called friend adds, "Man, I know you ain't got a cent to your name."

And he's right, you don't. But you got your freedom. Remember your new middle name?

So what do you do?

You pass again.

Why?

Because the man who owes the debt will see your presence as an attempt to intimidate, and he will pull a gun on you or call the police. And he'll have you on camera.

So what is there to do? Endure the pain of the transition, stay off drugs, go to work as soon as you can, go to school to learn new skills, and reconnect with your family or start your own. You can do it.

If you ever doubt it, remember your new middle name.

And when you get a chance, drop a note to your old friends that stayed behind in prison. Those who helped you out and are working to be free one day. Tell them about your struggles and your successes. They will appreciate it, for you will inspire them, and you will add new meaning to your life.

Letter to a Prisoner 28

Hope

You don't want to ever give up. Even if they gave you five life sentences to serve consecutively—you have to die before starting to serve the next one and so on. But there are two sides to hope. One is passive and the other active.

There are lots of people out there right now, strong people, diligent and committed men and women, who are doing a great deal to improve prison conditions. And the results are coming in, a little at a time, but they are coming in. These folks are doing the work. You are not.

The active side of hope concerns you. What are you doing to improve prison conditions? What are you doing to get along better with the guards?

True, the setting could be more conducive to rich human interactions, but that is the world as it is. If Lincoln hadn't been assassinated, or Martin Luther King, then we probably would be seeing different prison populations and different settings. But they were.

The men and women now helping to change things are great believers in advancing the human project, driven by the notion that earlier mistakes can and should be corrected, and that there is an urgent need to do so. They are trying hard to convince the rest of society that you are worth paying attention to, and that in the end we will all benefit from such changes. But they need help, and they need help from you.

How do you help? By making every effort possible to decrease violence in prison.

Imagine for a moment, that there arose amongst you a collective desire for renewal, a desire for greater tolerance, a willingness to accept your responsibility in any conflict, to stop blaming, to address differences with parleys rather than fists and kicks and knives and riots. What message would you be sending to the world outside? That you can rise to learn to nurture each other. That you are willing to invest in your community, so you can guide and mediate, teach and redirect energies. As you do, you would be sending to all who are not deaf, a message that says, "come close and see that men who have failed can change."

It is not for lack of manpower that this is not happening, for there are presently, in your midst, bright men capable of stirring such efforts, men who have learned from their mistakes and who are more than ready to live productive lives. What has been missing is the commitment. And it will be needed to harness the willingness of many to join in, to step forward and forge alliances with custody and mental health.

A newspaper would help. Every prison should have one, for it encourages people to learn to use thought and the power of persuasion through the debate of ideas. But for it to work, there has to be a genuine desire to accept responsibility and the courage to learn to live in harmony.

Acknowledgments

My thanks to my esteemed colleague Vasudha Ahuja, MD, who graciously took the time to read the manuscript and offer her impressions. The final product is entirely my responsibility.

My thanks also to my fellow psychiatrists, clinicians, custody, and staff at the Los Angeles County State Prison in Lancaster, California, for the support I was given during the years I worked there, December 2010 through December 2016.

Previously, I had worked at the California Institute for Men in Chino and Wasco State Prison. I am equally grateful to them for the support that was extended to me.

About the Author

Oscar Valdes has worked in the theatre and written lyrics. His novel, *Walk Through Your Shadows,* will be out in the fall of 2017.

Author photo © Masashi Nagadoi

www.ingramcontent.com/pod-product-compliance
Lightning Source LLC
Chambersburg PA
CBHW020700300426
44112CB00007B/462